This book belongs to

............Baby Isaak...............

I can't wait to meet you!
Here's to many wonderful
bedtime stones in the years ahead.
Lots of love.
xo, Sam Cohen

This is a Parragon Publishing Book
This edition published in 2006

Parragon Publishing
Queen Street House
4 Queen Street
Bath BA1 1HE, UK

Copyright © Parragon Books Ltd 2001

Created by small world creations ltd
Printed in China
ISBN 1-40545-361-3

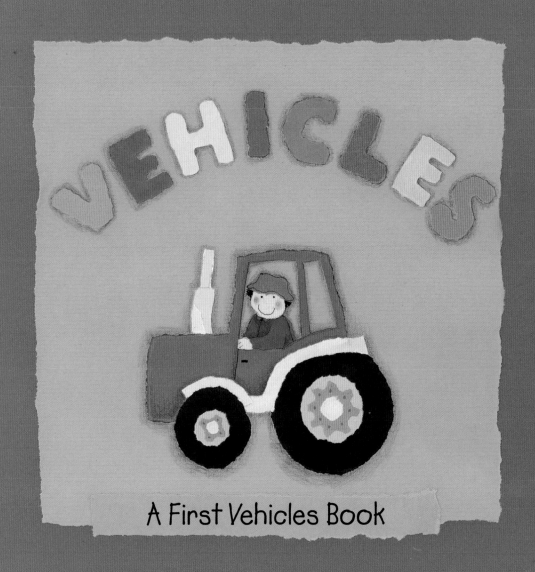

VEHICLES

A First Vehicles Book

p

car

Here comes a big

Beep, beep!

red racing car!

bike

Tring!
Tring!

My shiny new bicycle
has a silver bell.

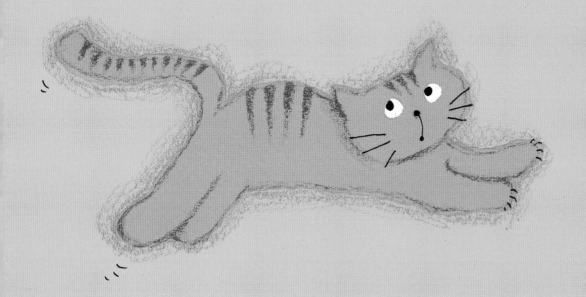

fire truck

This fire truck has
a flashing blue light

and a **very loud** siren.

tractor

Tractors have great big wheels

Chug! Chug!

for driving over muddy fields.

train

Make way for the train!

Chug, chug! Toot, toot!

boats

Look at all these colorful

boats bobbing on the waves.

digger

This digger is making

bus

"Two tickets home, please."

Ding, ding!

truck

This truck can carry

lots of heavy furniture.

motorbike

VROOM!
goes the motorbike
as it whizzes by.

airplane

WHOOSH!

The airplane flies

high above the clouds.